SOMEWHERE IS
SUCH A KINGDOM

SOMEWHERE IS SUCH A KINGDOM

POEMS 1952-1971

Geoffrey Hill

with an introduction
by Harold Bloom

1975

HOUGHTON MIFFLIN COMPANY BOSTON

First American Edition 1975
Introduction copyright © 1975 by Harold Bloom
Copyright © 1959, 1964, 1968, 1971, 1975
by Geoffrey Hill. All rights reserved.
Library of Congress Cataloging in Publication Data
Hill, Geoffrey
Somewhere is such a kingdom.
CONTENTS: For the unfallen (1959) — King Log (1968). —.
Mercian hymns. (1971). I. Title.
PR6015.I4735S6   821'.9'14   75-11949
ISBN 0-395-20713-4
ISBN 0-395-20712-6 pbk.
Printed in the United States of America

c 9 8 7 6 5 4 3 2 1

Sometimes a man seeks what he hath lost; and from that place, and time, wherein he misses it, his mind runs back, from place to place, and time to time, to find where, and when he had it . . .

Thomas Hobbes, Leviathan, *1651.*

Notes & Acknowledgments

Somewhere Is Such a Kingdom: Poems 1952-1971 brings together three previous volumes: *For the Unfallen* (1959), *King Log* (1968), and *Mercian Hymns* (1971), all published in the U.K. by Andre Deutsch Limited. In the individual British editions, *For the Unfallen* is dedicated to Nancy Hill and *King Log* to Kenneth Curtis.

The title of this book is the title of a poem by John Crowe Ransom. I gratefully acknowledge this debt.

The six lines from Allen Tate's "More Sonnets at Christmas, 1942" (p. 36) are quoted from *Poems* by Allen Tate, by kind permission of the author and of The Swallow Press.

"In Memory of Jane Fraser" (p. 11) is here reprinted with the revised final stanza, as in the third (1971) impression of *For the Unfallen.*

Contents

KING LOG (1968)

Introduction

THE SURVIVAL OF STRONG POETRY

STRONG POETRY is always difficult, and Geoffrey Hill is the strongest British poet now alive, though his reputation in the English-speaking world is somewhat less advanced than that of several of his contemporaries. He should be read and studied for many generations after they have blended together, just as he should survive all but a handful (or fewer) of American poets now active. Such canonic prophecy is founded on the authority of his best work, as I have experienced it in the fifteen years since the publication of *For the Unfallen*, his first book. From his first poem, appropriately "Genesis," on through the *Mercian Hymns*, Hill has been the most Blakean of modern poets. But this is deep or true influence, or Blake's Mental Warfare, rather than the easy transmission of image, idea, diction, and metric that superficially is judged to be poetic influence. The merely extrinsic influences on Hill's early verses are mostly American; I can detect the fierce rhetoric of Allen Tate, and the visionary intensities of Richard Eberhart, in some places. Yet the true precursor is always Blake, and the War in Heaven that the strong poet must conduct is fought by Hill against Blake, and against Blake's tradition, and so against Hill himself.

As a war of poetry against poetry, Hill's work testifies to the repressive power of tradition, but also to an immensely individual and deeply moving moral protest against tradition. Like the hero he celebrates in his masterpiece, the *Mercian Hymns*, Hill is a martyrologist. His subject is human pain, the suffering of those who both do and sustain violence, and more exactly the daemonic relationship between cultural tradition and human pain. Confronted by Hill's best poems, a reader is at first tempted to turn away, for the intellectual difficulty of the rugged, compressed verse is more than matched by the emotional painfulness and directness of Hill's vision. Hill does not comfort nor console, and offers no dialectic of gain through loss. His subject, like his style, is difficulty: the difficulty of apprehending and accepting moral guilt, and the difficulty of being a poet when the burden of history, including poetic history, makes any prophetic stance inauthentic. In more than twenty years of writing, Hill has given us three very slim volumes, not because his gift is sparse, but because he is too scrupulous to have allowed himself a less organized or less weighted utterance. There are no bad poems in Hill's three books, and so much is demanded of the reader, in concentration and in the dignity of a desperate humanism, that more productive poets are likely to seem too indulgent by comparison. Hill does not indulge his reader, or himself, and just this remorseless concentration is Hill's assured greatness. The reader who persists will learn to read not only Hill but other difficult and wholly indispensable poets as well, for only a poet as strong as Hill compels each of us to test his own strength as a reader, and so to test and clarify also our own relation to tradition.

Tradition, Freud surmised, was the cultural equivalent of repressed material in the consciousness of the individual. The role of repression in poetry was misunderstood by Freud and has been misunderstood by most of his followers. Freud thought that sublimation was the psychic defense that *worked*, whether in life or in literature, while repression invariably failed, since repression augmented the unconscious. But poetry *is* figurative language, and in poetry sublimation is accomplished through the self-limiting trope of metaphor, while repression is represented by the expansive trope of hyperbole, with all of its Sublime glories and Grotesque dangers. From the viewpoint of poetry, the "unconscious mind" is an oxymoron, since repressed material in poetry has no place to go but up, onto the heights of what Romanticism called the Imagination. Romantic Imagination, whether in Blake or Coleridge, does not represent a return of the repressed, but is identical with the process of repression itself.

An individual poetic imagination can defend itself against the force of another imagination only by troping, so that a successful defense against poetic tradition always answers repression by an increase in repression. The return of the repressed is only a utopian or apocalyptic dream much indulged in by Marxist speculation and by assorted contemporary shamans who inspire what is still being termed a counterculture. Authentic poets show us that Emersonian Compensation is always at work in poetry as in life: nothing is got for nothing. What returns in authentic poetry is never the repressed, but rather the daemonic or uncanny element within repression, which poetic tradition has called by various names, including the Sublime and the Imagination, both of them hyperbolical figurations for something that has no referential aspect or literal meaning but that nevertheless guarantees the survival and continuity of poetic tradition. Poets and readers go on questing for one another in order to give a voice to this daemonic impulse that informs and purifies repression. "Purifies" here has no moral or spiritual meaning but refers rather to a process by which the daemonic is reconciled with the writing of poetry.

"Daemonic," in this sense, refers to a realm of power that invades the human world yet seems apart from human origins or human ends. In a very early poem, a visionary lyric in the mode of Eberhart, but like Eberhart reaching back to Blake's *Tyger*, Hill laments the inadequacy of poetic language to tell his own experience of daemonic influx:

> *I waited for the word that was not given,*
>
> *Pent up into a region of pure force,*
> *Made subject to the pressure of the stars;*
> *I saw the angels lifted like pale straws;*
> *I could not stand before those winnowing eyes*
>
> *And fell, until I found the world again.*

Hill dislikes his early poems, yet they are not only permanent achievements but also quite essential for understanding all that comes after. "Genesis," for which he has a particular dislike, is superb in itself, a perfect "first" poem and also a clear intimation of his largest debt to Blake's vision, which is the conviction that the Creation and the Fall were the same event. Another fine early poem, "In Memory of Jane Fraser" (which Hill evidently dislikes most, of all his work), speaks of a single, particular death as uncreating all of nature. For Hill, the natural world is, at best, "a stunned repose," a judgment that allies him to Blake rather than to Wordsworth, Shelley rather than to Keats. Hill's poem on the death of Shelley emphasizes the survival of the animal world, even as Shelley, the Modern Poet proper, or New Perseus, quests aimlessly, "clogged sword, clear, aimless mirror — / With nothing to strike at or blind / in the frothed shallows."

The themes and procedures of both Hill's books of short poems are summed up in what I judge to be his best single poem, the double-sonnet called "Annunciations." Though Hill transcends his own earlier mode in *Mercian Hymns* (as will be seen), "Annunciations" is so important a poem that I will discuss it at some length. A reader who can interpret "Annunciations" can learn to interpret the rest of Hill, and also acquire many insights that will aid in reading any truly difficult poetry of the post-Romantic tradition. For, in "Annunciations," Hill wrote what later tradition may judge to have been the central shorter poem of his own generation, a poem that is itself a despairing poetics, and a total vision both of natural existence, and of the necessary limitations of what we have learned to call imagination.

An "annunciation" can be any proclamation, but despite Hill's plural title, the reverberation here depends upon the Annunciation proper, the announcement of the Incarnation by the Angel Gabriel in Luke 1:26-38. In some grim sense Hill's starting point is the festival (March 25) celebrating Gabriel's announcement. But "the Word" here is not the Logos, nor simply the words of poetry, all poetry, but the idealization of poetry that is so pervasive in Western tradition:

> *The Word has been abroad, is back, with a tanned look*
> *From its subsistence in the stiffening-mire.*
> *Cleansing has become killing, the reward*
> *Touchable, overt, clean to the touch.*

This Word seems more a tourist than an Eliotic explorer; indeed a hygienic hunter-tourist. Returned, the questers sit together at a literary feast with their scholarly and critical admirers:

> *Now at a distance from the steam of beasts,*
> *The loathly neckings and fat shook spawn*
> *(Each specimen-jar fed with delicate spawn)*
> *The searchers with the curers sit at meat*
> *And are satisfied.*

I do not know how to interpret this except as an attack upon everyone who has to do with poetry: poets, critics, teachers, students, readers. It is as though Yeats, after observing in vision his nymphs and satyrs copulating in the foam, his Innocents reliving their pain and having their wounds opened again, then attended a banquet in honor of his "News for the Delphic Oracle." The poem becomes a "specimen-jar," holding an aesthetic reduction of copulation and bleeding wounds. Is such an attack as Hill's legitimate, since it would apply as much to Homer as to any other poet? Is Hill attacking a false idealization of poetry or the *Ananke* that governs all poetry? The remainder of the first part of "Annunciations" will not answer these questions:

> *Such precious things put down*
> *And the flesh eased through turbulence the soul*
> *Purples itself; each eye squats full and mild*
> *While all who attend to fiddle or to harp*
> *For betterment, flavour their decent mouths*
> *With gobbets of the sweetest sacrifice.*

Primarily this is Hill's uncompromising attack upon himself, for even more than Yeats, or even his contemporary Ted Hughes, he writes a poetry whose subject is violence and pain, thus accepting the danger of easing the flesh through a vision of turbulence. Much of the success with readers, particularly British readers, of the later Yeats and of Hughes is surely based upon feeding the reader's eye with imaginary lust and suffering until that eye "squats full and mild." Hill's attack upon "all who attend to fiddle or to harp/ For betterment" is therefore an attack upon the most traditional, Aristotelian defense of poetry, an attack upon the supposed function of catharsis. Poems are "gobbets of the sweetest sacrifice," and readers flavor their mouths decently even as decent Christians swallow the bread of communion. It becomes clear that Hill is attacking, ultimately, neither poetry nor religion, but the inescapable element that always darkens tradition, which is that the living, feeding upon the repressions of the dead, repress further and so become the sustenance of the dead. Hill's "sacrifice" is what Nietzsche and Freud would have termed an Antithetical Primal Word, for it is debatable whether the victims commemorated by the poem, or the readers, are the "sacrifice."

The Antithetical Primal Word of the second part of "Annunciations" is of course "love," and here the majestic bitterness of the Sublime triumphs in and over Hill:

> O Love, subject of the mere diurnal grind,
> Forever being pledged to be redeemed,
> Expose yourself for charity; be assured
> The body is but husk and excrement.
> Enter these deaths according to the law,
> O visited women, possessed sons! Foreign lusts
> Infringe our restraints; the changeable
> Soldiery have their goings-out and comings-in
> Dying in abundance. Choicest beasts
> Suffuse the gutters with their colourful blood.
> Our God scatters corruption. Priests, martyrs,

Parade to this imperious theme: 'O Love,
You know what pains succeed; be vigilant; strive
To recognize the damned among your friends.'

If I could cite only one stanza by Hill as being wholly representative of him, it would be this, for here is his power, his despair, and (in spite of himself) his Word, not in the sense of Logos but in the Hebraic sense of *davhar*, a word that is also an act, a bringing-forward of something previously held back in the self. This Word that rejects being a Word is a knowing misprision or mistaking of tradition, but even the most revisionary of Words remains a Word, as Hill doubtless knows. Being willing to go on writing poems, however sparsely, is to believe that one possesses a Word of one's own to bring forward. When Hill says, "Our God scatters corruption," he means that the God of lovers (and of poets) is antithetical to Himself, that this God is the ambivalent deity of all Gnostics. I take it that "scatters" does not mean "drives away" but rather "increases" corruption by dispersal, which implies that "corruption" takes something of its root meaning of "broken-to-pieces." Hill's subject then is the Gnostic or Kabbalistic "Breaking of the Vessels," the Fall that is simultaneously a Creation, as in his first, Blakean, chant-poem "Genesis."

Part II of "Annunciations" is thus more of a proclamation against Love than a prayer to Love. Love, addressed under its aspect of repetition, is urged to more honesty, and to a reductive awareness of the body. Corporeal passion lives and dies according to the old dispensation, or law, but Hill comes to proclaim a new Incarnation, which is only a Gnostic dying into yet more sexual abundance. As an incessant martyrologist, Hill grimly announces the imperious as against the imperial or Shakespearean theme. Love, who knows that pains only succeed or follow one another (but are never successful), is urged at least to distinguish its true martyrs among the panoply of the worshipers, and so recognize accurately its valid theme.

Repeated readings of "Annunciations" should clarify and justify Hill's densely impacted style, with its reliance upon figurations of hyperbole. Hill's mode is a negative or counter-Sublime, and his characteristic defense against the tradition he beautifully sustains and extends is an almost primal repression:

> *Not as we are but as we must appear,*
> *Contractual ghosts of pity; not as we*
> *Desire life but as they would have us live,*
> *Set apart in timeless colloquy:*
> *So it is required; so we bear witness,*
> *Despite ourselves, to what is beyond us,*
> *Each distant sphere of harmony forever*
> *Poised, unanswerable . . .*

This is again a Gnostic sublimity. Blake could still insist that pity survived only because we kept on rendering others piteous, but Hill comes later, and for him the intoxication of belatedness is to know that our reality and our desire are both negated by our appearance as legatees. It is tradition that makes us into "contractual ghosts of pity." A Beautiful Necessity represses us and makes us bear witness to a dead but still powerful transcendence. Hill characterizes one of his sequences as "a florid grim music" or an "ornate and heartless music punctuated by mutterings, blasphemies and cries for help." A baroque pathos seems to be Hill's goal, with the ornateness his tribute to tradition and the punctuation of pathos his outcry against tradition. Hill's is clearly a poetics of pain, in which all the calamities of history become so many poetic salutes, so many baroque meditations, always trapped in a single repetition of realization. Man is trapped "between the stones and the void," without majesty and without justice except for the errors of rhetoric, the illusions of poetic language. Like his own Sebastian Arrurruz, Hill's task is "to find value/ In a bleak skill," the poet's craft of establishing true rather than false "sequences of pain."

"It must give pleasure," Stevens rightly insisted, and any critic responding to Hill should be prepared to say how and why Hill's poetry can give pleasure, and in what sense Hill's reader can defend himself from being only another decent mouth opened wide for the poetry-banquet. How is the reader to evade becoming "the (supposed) Patron" so bitterly invoked in the final poem of Hill's first book? The Gnostic answer, which is always a latecomer's answer, is that the reader must become not a patron but one of those unfallen who gave Hill's first book its title:

> For the unfallen — the firstborn, or wise
> Councillor — prepared vistas extend
> As far as harvest; and idyllic death
> Where fish at dawn ignite the powdery lake.

The final trope here is perhaps too Yeatsian, but the previous trope that gives back priority to the unfallen has a more High Romantic tenor, looking back to Keats's vision of autumn. Hill cannot celebrate natural completion, but he always finds himself turning again "to flesh and blood and the blood's pain" despite his Gnostic desire to renounce for good "this fierce and unregenerate clay." Of his incessant ambivalence, Hill has made a strong poetry, one that battles tradition on tradition's own terms, and that attempts to make of the poet's conscious belatedness an earliness. The accomplished reader responds to Hill's work as to any really strong poetry, for the reader too needs to put off his own belatedness, which is surely why we go on searching for strong poetry. We cannot live with tradition, and we cannot live without it, and so we turn to the strong poet to see how he acts out this ambivalence for us, and to see also if he can get beyond such ambivalence.

Hill begins to break through his own dialectics of tradition in *Mercian Hymns*, the sequence of prose-poems he published on the threshold of turning forty. His hero is Offa, an eighth-century Midlands "king," who merges both into a spirit of place and into the poet celebrating him, particularly the poet-as-schoolboy, for *Mercian Hymns* is a kind of *Prelude*-in-little. Yet here the growth of a poet's mind is not stimulated by nature's teachings, but only by history and by dreams. Transcendence, for Hill, returned or reentered the sublunary world in old tapestries, sculpture, and metalwork, but mostly in historicizing reverie, which is the substance of these hymns. With *Mercian Hymns*, Hill rather triumphantly "makes it new," and though the obsession with tradition is as strong, much of the ambivalence toward tradition is miraculously diminished. Indeed, certain passages in *Mercian Hymns* would approach sentimentality if the poet did not remain characteristically condensed and gnomic, with the familiar specter of pain hovering uncannily close:

> *We have a kitchen-garden riddled with toy-shards, with splinters of habitation. The children shriek and scavenge, play havoc. They incinerate boxes, rags and old tyres. They haul a sodden log, hung with soft shields of fungus, and launch it upon the flames.*

Difficult as Hill was earlier, *Mercian Hymns*, despite the limpidity of its individual sections, is the subtlest and most oblique of his works. It is not only hard to hold together, but there is some question as to what it is "about," though the necessary answer is akin to *The Prelude* again; Hill has at last no subject but his own complex subjectivity, and so the poem is "about" himself, which turns out to be his exchange of gifts with the Muse of History (Section X). I suggest that the structure and meaning of *Mercian Hymns* is best approached through its rhetoric, which as before in Hill is largely that of metaleptic reversal or transumption, the dominant trope of post-Romantic poetry in English. For a full analysis of the trope and its poetic history, I must refer to my book, *A Map of Misreading* and give only a brief account here. Transumption is the trope of a trope, or technically the metonymy of a metonymy. That is, it tends to be a figure that substitutes an aspect of a previous figure for that figure. Imagistically, transumption from Milton through the Romantics to the present tends to manifest itself in terms of earliness substituting for lateness, and more often than not to be the figure that concludes poems. Translated into psychoanalytic terms, transumption is either the psychic defense of introjection (identification) or of projection (refusal of identity), just as metaphor translates into the defense of sublimation, or hyperbole into that of repression. The advantage of transumption as a concluding trope for belated poems is that it achieves a kind of fresh priority or earliness, but always at the expense of the presentness of the present or living moment. Hill is as transumptive a poet, rhetorically, as Milton or Wordsworth or Wallace Stevens, and so he too is unable to celebrate a present joy.

There is no present time, indeed there is no self-presence in *Mercian Hymns*. Though Hill's own note on the sequence betrays some anxiety about what he calls anachronisms, the genius of his work excludes such anxiety. Nothing can be anachronistic when there is no present:

> *King of the perennial holly-groves, the riven sand-*
> *stone: overlord of the M5: architect of the*
> *historic rampart and ditch, the citadel at Tam-*
> *worth, the summer hermitage in Holy Cross:*
> *guardian of the Welsh Bridge and the Iron*
> *Bridge: contractor to the desirable new estates:*
> *saltmaster: money-changer: commissioner for*
> *oaths: martyrologist: the friend of Charlemagne.*

'*I liked that,*' *said Offa,* '*sing it again.*'

It is not that Offa has returned to merge with the poet, or that Hill has gone back to Offa. Hill and Offa stand together in a figuration that has introjected the past and the future, while projecting the present. Hill's epigraph, from the neglected poet and essayist C. H. Sisson, analogizes his own conduct as private person and Offa's conduct of government, in all aspects of conduct having to do with "object and justification." Hill's struggle, as person and as poet, is with the repressive power of tradition, with the anxieties of history. Offa is seen by Hill as "the starting-cry of a race," as the master of a Primal Scene of Instruction, an imposition of order that fixates subsequent repression in others, which means to start an inescapable tradition. By reconciling himself with Offa, Hill comes close to accepting the necessary violence of tradition that earlier had induced enormous ambivalences in his poetry.

This acceptance, still somber but no longer grim, produces the dominant tone of *Mercian Hymns*, which is a kind of Wordsworthian "sober coloring" or "still sad music of humanity." But the sequence's vision remains Blakean rather than Wordsworthian, for the world it pictures is still one in which Creation and Fall cannot be distinguished, and at the end Offa is fallen Adam or every man: "he left behind coins, for his lodging, and traces of red mud." The reader sees that each hymn is like the inscription on one of Offa's hammered coins, and that these coins are literally and figuratively the price of a living tradition, its perpetual balance of Creation and Fall. Hill has succeeded, obliquely, in solving his aesthetic-moral problem as a poet, but the success is as equivocal and momentary as the pun on "succeed" in "Annunciations." Hill now knows better "what pains succeed," and his moving sequence helps his readers to the same knowledge.

No critical introduction to a poet only just past forty in age can hope to prophesy his future development. I have seen no poems written by Hill since *Mercian Hymns*, but would be surprised if he did not return to the tighter mode of *For the Unfallen* and *King Log*, though in a finer tone. He has the persistence to go on wrestling with the mighty dead — Blake, Wordsworth,

Shelley, Yeats — and to make of this ghostly struggle a fresh sub-limity. He is indeed a poet of the Sublime, a mode wholly archaic yet always available to us again, provided a survivor of the old line comes to us:

> *Against the burly air I strode,*
> *Where the tight ocean heaves its load,*
> *Crying the miracles of God.*

HAROLD BLOOM

FOR THE UNFALLEN

GENESIS

I

Against the burly air I strode,
Where the tight ocean heaves its load,
Crying the miracles of God.

And first I brought the sea to bear
Upon the dead weight of the land;
And the waves flourished at my prayer,
The rivers spawned their sand.

And where the streams were salt and full
The tough pig-headed salmon strove,
Curbing the ebb and the tide's pull,
To reach the steady hills above.

II

The second day I stood and saw
The osprey plunge with triggered claw,
Feathering blood along the shore,
To lay the living sinew bare.

And the third day I cried: 'Beware
The soft-voiced owl, the ferret's smile,
The hawk's deliberate stoop in air,
Cold eyes, and bodies hooped in steel,
Forever bent upon the kill.'

III

And I renounced, on the fourth day,
This fierce and unregenerate clay,

Building as a huge myth for man
The watery Leviathan,

And made the glove-winged albatross
Scour the ashes of the sea
Where Capricorn and Zero cross,
A brooding immortality –
Such as the charmed phoenix has
In the unwithering tree.

IV

The phoenix burns as cold as frost;
And, like a legendary ghost,
The phantom-bird goes wild and lost,
Upon a pointless ocean tossed.

So, the fifth day, I turned again
To flesh and blood and the blood's pain.

V

On the sixth day, as I rode
In haste about the works of God,
With spurs I plucked the horse's blood.

By blood we live, the hot, the cold,
To ravage and redeem the world:
There is no bloodless myth will hold.

And by Christ's blood are men made free
Though in close shrouds their bodies lie
Under the rough pelt of the sea;

Though Earth has rolled beneath her weight
The bones that cannot bear the light.

GOD'S LITTLE MOUNTAIN

Below, the river scrambled like a goat
Dislodging stones. The mountain stamped its foot,
Shaking, as from a trance. And I was shut
With wads of sound into a sudden quiet.

I thought the thunder had unsettled heaven,
All was so still. And yet the sky was cloven
By flame that left the air cold and engraven.
I waited for the word that was not given,

Pent up into a region of pure force,
Made subject to the pressure of the stars;
I saw the angels lifted like pale straws;
I could not stand before those winnowing eyes

And fell, until I found the world again.
Now I lack grace to tell what I have seen;
For though the head frames words the tongue has none.
And who will prove the surgeon to this stone?

HOLY THURSDAY

Naked, he climbed to the wolf's lair;
He beheld Eden without fear,
Finding no ambush offered there
But sleep under the harbouring fur.

He said: 'They are decoyed by love
Who, tarrying through the hollow grove,
Neglect the seasons' sad remove.
Child and nurse walk hand in glove

As unaware of Time's betrayal,
Weaving their innocence with guile.
But they must cleave the fire's peril
And suffer innocence to fall.

I have been touched with that fire,
And have fronted the she-wolf's lair.
Lo, she lies gentle and innocent of desire
Who was my constant myth and terror.'

MERLIN

I will consider the outnumbering dead:
For they are the husks of what was rich seed.
Now, should they come together to be fed,
They would outstrip the locusts' covering tide.

Arthur, Elaine, Mordred; they are all gone
Among the raftered galleries of bone.
By the long barrows of Logres they are made one,
And over their city stands the pinnacled corn.

THE BIDDEN GUEST

The starched unbending candles stir
As though a wind had caught their hair,
As though the surging of a host
Had charged the air of Pentecost.
And I believe in the spurred flame,
Those racing tongues, but cannot come
Out of my heart's unbroken room;
Nor feel the lips of fire among
The cold light and the chilling song,
The broken mouths that spill their hoard
Of prayer like beads on to a board.
There, at the rail, each muffled head
Swings sombrely. O quiet deed!
This is the breaking of the bread;
On this the leanest heart may feed
When by the stiffly-linened priest
All wounds of light are newly dressed,
Healed by the pouring-in of wine
From bitter – as from sweet – grapes bled.
But one man lay beneath his vine
And, waking, found that it was dead.
And so my heart has ceased to breathe
(Though there God's worm blunted its head
And stayed.) And still I seem to smile.
Wounds have thick lips and cannot tell
If there is blackness couched beneath.
'Yet there are wounds, unquenched with oil,
And blazing eyes that would compel
Evil to turn, though, like a mole
It dug blind alleys down the soil.'

So I heard once. But now I hear,
Like shifted blows at my numb back,
A grinding heel; a scraped chair.
The heart's tough shell is still to crack
When, spent of all its wine and bread,
Unwinkingly the altar lies
Wreathed in its sour breath, cold and dead.
A server has put out its eyes.

IN MEMORY OF JANE FRASER

When snow like sheep lay in the fold
And winds went begging at each door,
And the far hills were blue with cold,
And a cold shroud lay on the moor,

She kept the siege. And every day
We watched her brooding over death
Like a strong bird above its prey.
The room filled with the kettle's breath.

Damp curtains glued against the pane
Sealed time away. Her body froze
As if to freeze us all, and chain
Creation to a stunned repose.

She died before the world could stir.
In March the ice unloosed the brook
And water ruffled the sun's hair.
Dead cones upon the alder shook.

THE TURTLE DOVE

Love that drained her drained him she'd loved, though each
For the other's sake forged passion upon speech,
Bore their close days through sufferance towards night
Where she at length grasped sleep and he lay quiet

As though needing no questions, now, to guess
What her secreting heart could not well hide.
Her caught face flinched in half-sleep at his side.
Yet she, by day, modelled her real distress,

Poised, turned her cheek to the attending world
Of children and intriguers and the old,
Conversed freely, exercised, was admired,
Being strong to dazzle. All this she endured

To affront him. He watched her rough grief work
Under the formed surface of habit. She spoke
Like one long undeceived but she was hurt.
She denied more love, yet her starved eyes caught

His, devouring, at times. Then, as one self-dared,
She went to him, plied there; like a furious dove
Bore down with visitations of such love
As his lithe, fathoming heart absorbed and buried.

THE TROUBLESOME REIGN

So much he had from fashion and no more:
Her trained hard gaze, brief lips whose laughter spat
Concession to desire – she suffered that,
Feeding a certain green-fuel to his fire.

Reluctant heat! This burning of the dead
Could consume her also; she moved apart
As if, through such denial, he might be made
Himself again familiar and unscarred,

Contained, even wary, though not too much
To take pleasure considering her flesh shone,
Her salt-worn summer dress. But he had gone
Thirty days through such a dream of taste and touch

When the sun stood for him and the violent larks
Stabbed up into the sun. She was his, then;
Her limbs grasped him, satisfied, while his brain
Judged every move and cry from its separate dark.

More dark, more separate, now, yet still not dead,
Their mouths being drawn to public and private speech –
Though there was too much care in all he said,
A hard kind of no-feeling in her touch –

By such rites they saved love's face, and such laws
As prescribe mutual tolerance, charity
To neighbours, strangers, those by nature
Subdued among famines and difficult wars.

SOLOMON'S MINES

To Bonamy Dobrée

Anything to have done!
(The eagle flagged to the sun)
To have discovered and disclosed
The buried thrones, the means used;

Spadework and symbol; each deed
Resurrecting those best dead
Priests, soldiers and kings;
Blazed-out, stripped-out things;

Anything to get up and go
(Let the hewn gates clash to)
Without looking round
Out of that strong land.

THE DISTANT FURY OF BATTLE

Grass resurrects to mask, to strangle,
Words glossed on stone, lopped stone-angel;
But the dead maintain their ground –
That there's no getting round –

Who in places vitally rest,
Named, anonymous; who test
Alike the endurance of yews
Laurels, moonshine, stone, all tissues;

With whom, under licence and duress,
There are pacts made, if not peace.
Union with the stone-wearing dead
Claims the born leader, the prepared

Leader, the devourers and all lean men.
Some, finally, learn to begin.
Some keep to the arrangement of love
(Or similar trust) under whose auspices move

Most subjects, toward the profits of this
Combine of doves and witnesses.
Some, dug out of hot-beds, are brought bare,
Not past conceiving but past care.

ASMODEUS

I

They, after the slow building of the house,
Furnished it; brought warmth under the skin.
Tiles, that a year's rough wind could rattle loose,
Being close-pressed still kept storms out and storms in.
(Of all primed and vain citadels, to choose
This, to choose this of all times to begin!)
Acknowledging, they said, one who pursues
Hobbies of serious lust and indoor sin,
Clearly they both stood, lovers without fear,
Might toy with fire brought dangerously to hand
To tame, not exorcise, spirits; though the air
Whistled abstracted menace, could confound
Strength by device, by music reaching the ear,
Lightning conducted forcibly to the ground.

II

The night, then; bravely stiffen; you are one
Whom stars could burn more deeply than the sun,
Guide-book martyr. You, doubtless, hear wings,
Too sheer for cover, swift; the scattered noise
Of darkness looming with propitious things;
And nests of rumour clustered in the world.
So drummed, so shadowed, your mere trudging voice
Might rave at large while easy truths were told,
Bad perjurable stuff, to be forgiven
Because of this lame journey out of mind.
A tax on men to seventy-times-seven,
A busy vigilance of goose and hound,
Keeps up all guards. Since you are outside, go,
Closing the doors of the house and the head also.

REQUIEM FOR THE
PLANTAGENET KINGS

For whom the possessed sea littered, on both shores,
Ruinous arms; being fired, and for good,
To sound the constitution of just wars,
Men, in their eloquent fashion, understood.

Relieved of soul, the dropping-back of dust,
Their usage, pride, admitted within doors;
At home, under caved chantries, set in trust,
With well-dressed alabaster and proved spurs
They lie; they lie; secure in the decay
Of blood, blood-marks, crowns hacked and coveted,
Before the scouring fires of trial-day
Alight on men; before sleeked groin, gored head,
Budge through the clay and gravel, and the sea
Across daubed rock evacuates its dead.

TWO FORMAL ELEGIES

For the Jews in Europe

I

Knowing the dead, and how some are disposed:
Subdued under rubble, water, in sand graves,
In clenched cinders not yielding their abused
Bodies and bonds to those whom war's chance saves
Without the law: we grasp, roughly, the song.
Arrogant acceptance from which song derives
Is bedded with their blood, makes flourish young
Roots in ashes. The wilderness revives,

Deceives with sweetness harshness. Still beneath
Live skin stone breathes, about which fires but play,
Fierce heart that is the iced brain's to command
To judgment – (studied reflex, contained breath) –
Their best of worlds since, on the ordained day,
This world went spinning from Jehovah's hand.

For all that must be gone through, their long death
Documented and safe, we have enough
Witnesses (our world being witness-proof).
The sea flickers, roars, in its wide hearth.
Here, yearly, the pushing midlanders stand
To warm themselves; men, brawny with life,
Women who expect life. They relieve
Their thickening bodies, settle on scraped sand.

Is it good to remind them, on a brief screen,
Of what they have witnessed and not seen?
(Deaths of the city that persistently dies . . .?)
To put up stones ensures some sacrifice.
Sufficient men confer, carry their weight.
(At whose door does the sacrifice stand or start?)

METAMORPHOSES

I The Fear

No manner of address will do;
Eloquence is not in that look,
But fear of a furred kind. You
Display the stiff face of shock.

Hate is not in it, nor that
Which has presence, a character
In civil intercourse – deceit
Of a tough weathering-nature.

This fear strikes hard and is gone
And is recognised when found
Not only between dark and dawn,
The summit and the ground.

Through scant pride to be so put out!
But feed, feed, unlyrical scapegoat;
Plague shrines where each fissure blows
Odour of laurel clouding yours!

Exercise, loftily, your visions
Where the mountainous distance
Echoes its unfaltering speech
To mere outcry and harrowing search.

Possessed of agility and passion,
Energy (out-of-town-fashion)
Attack every obstacle
And height; make the sun your pedestal.

Settle all that bad blood;
Be visited, touched, understood;
Be graced, groomed, returned to favour
With admirable restraint and fervour!

III The Re-birth of Venus

And now the sea-scoured temptress, having failed
To scoop out of horizons what birds herald:
Tufts of fresh soil: shakes off an entire sea,
Though not as the dove, harried. Rather, she,

A shark hurricaned to estuary-water,
(The lesser hunter almost by a greater
Devoured) but unflurried, lies, approaches all
Stayers, and searchers of the fanged pool.

IV Drake's Drum

Those varied dead! The undiscerning sea
Shelves and dissolves their flesh as it burns spray

Who do not shriek like gulls nor dolphins ride
Crouched under spume to England's erect side

Though there a soaked sleeve lolls or shoe patrols
Tide-padded thick shallows, squats in choked pools

Neither our designed wreaths nor used words
Sink to their melted ears and melted hearts.

V

Doubtless he saw some path clear, having found
His love now fenced him off from the one ground
Where, as he owned, no temperate squalls could move
Either from the profession of their love.

Storm-bound, now she'd outweather him, though he,
Between sun-clouded marshworld and strewn sea
Pitched to extremities, in the rock's vein
Gripped for the winds to roughen and tide stain.

But when he tore his flesh-root and was gone,
Leaving no track, no blood gritting the stone,
Drawn freely to the darkness he had fought
Driven by sulphurous blood and a clenched heart,

Grant the detached, pierced spirit could plunge, soar,
Seeking that love flesh dared not answer for,
Nor suffers now, hammocked in salt tagged cloth
That to be bleached or burned the sea casts out.

PICTURE OF A NATIVITY

Sea-preserved, heaped with sea-spoils,
Ribs, keels, coral sores,
Detached faces, ephemeral oils,
Discharged on the world's outer shores,

A dumb child-king
Arrives at his right place; rests,
Undisturbed, among slack serpents; beasts
With claws flesh-buttered. In the gathering

Of bestial and common hardship
Artistic men appear to worship
And fall down; to recognise
Familiar tokens; believe their own eyes.

Above the marvel, each rigid head,
Angels, their unnatural wings displayed,
Freeze into an attitude
Recalling the dead.

CANTICLE FOR GOOD FRIDAY

The cross staggered him. At the cliff-top
Thomas, beneath its burden, stood
While the dulled wood
Spat on the stones each drop
Of deliberate blood.

A clamping, cold-figured day
Thomas (not transfigured) stamped, crouched,
Watched
Smelt vinegar and blood. He,
As yet unsearched, unscratched,

And suffered to remain
At such near distance
(A slight miracle might cleanse
His brain
Of all attachments, claw-roots of sense)

In unaccountable darkness moved away,
The strange flesh untouched, carrion-sustenance
Of staunchest love, choicest defiance,
Creation's issue congealing (and one woman's).

THE GUARDIANS

The young, having risen early, had gone,
Some with excursions beyond the bay-mouth,
Some toward lakes, a fragile reflected sun.
Thunder-heads drift, awkwardly, from the south;

The old watch them. They have watched the safe
Packed harbours topple under sudden gales,
Great tides irrupt, yachts burn at the wharf
That on clean seas pitched their effective sails.

There are silences. These, too, they endure:
Soft comings-on; soft after-shocks of calm.
Quietly they wade the disturbed shore;
Gather the dead as the first dead scrape home.

THE WHITE SHIP

Where the living with effort go,
Or with expense, the drowned wander
Easily: seaman
And king's son also

Who, by gross error lost,
Drift, now, in salt crushed
Polyp-and mackerel-fleshed
Tides between coast and coast,

Submerge or half-appear.
This does not much matter.
They are put down as dead. Water
Silences all who would interfere;

Retains, still, what it might give
As casually as it took away:
Creatures passed through the wet sieve
Without enrichment or decay.

WREATHS

I

Each day the tide withdraws; chills us; pastes
The sand with dead gulls, oranges, dead men.
Uttering love, that outlasts or outwastes
Time's attrition, exiles appear again,
But faintly altered in eyes and skin.

II

Into what understanding all have grown!
(Setting aside a few things, the still faces,
Climbing the phosphorus tide, that none will own)
What paradises and watering-places,
What hurts appeased by the sea's handsomeness!

ELEGIAC STANZAS

On a Visit to Dove Cottage

To J. P. Mann

Mountains, monuments, all forms
Inured to processes and storms
(And they are many); the fashions
Of intercourse between nations:

Customs through which many come
To sink their eyes into a room
Filled with the unused and unworn;
To bite nothings to the bone:

And the daylight between facts;
And the daylight between acts;
Groping of custom towards love;
Past loving, the custom to approve:

A use of words; a rhetoric
As plain as spitting on a stick;
Speech from the ice, the clear-obscure;
The tongue broody in the jaw:

Greatly-aloof, alert, rare
Spirit, conditioned to appear
At the authentic stone or seat:
O near-human spouse and poet,

Mountains, rivers, and grand storms,
Continuous profit, grand customs
(And many of them): O Lakes, Lakes!
O Sentiment upon the rocks!

AFTER CUMAE

The sun again unearthed, colours come up fresh,
The perennials; and the laurels'
Washable leaves, that seem never to perish,
Obscure the mouthy cave, the dumb grottoes.

From the beginning, in the known world, slide
Drawn echoing hulls, axes grate, and waves
Deposit in their shallow margins varied
Fragments of marine decay and waftage;

And the sometimes-abandoned gods confuse
With immortal essences men's brief lives,
Frequenting the exposed and pious: those
Who stray, as designed, under applied perils,

Whose doom is easy, venturing so far
Without need, other than to freeze or burn,
Their wake, on spread-out oceans, a healed scar
Fingered, themselves the curios of voyage.

LITTLE APOCALYPSE

Hölderlin: 1770–1843

Abrupt tempter; close enough to survive
The sun's primitive renewing fury;
Scorched vistas where crawl the injured and brave:
This man stands sealed against their injury:

Hermetic radiance of great suns kept in:
Man's common nature suddenly too rare:
See, for the brilliant coldness of his skin,
The god cast, perfected, among fire.

THE BIBLIOGRAPHERS

Lucifer blazing in superb effigies
Among the world's ambitious tragedies,
Heaven-sent gift to the dark ages,

Now, in the finest-possible light,
We approach you; can estimate
Your not unnatural height.

Though the discrete progeny,
Out of their swim, go deflated and dry,
We know the feel of you, archaic beauty,

Between the tombs, where the tombs still extrude,
Overshadowing the sun-struck world:
(The shadow-god envisaged in no cloud).

OF COMMERCE AND SOCIETY

Variations on a Theme

Then hang this picture for a calendar,
As sheep for goat, and pray most fixedly
For the cold martial progress of your star,
With thoughts of commerce and society,
Well-milked Chinese, Negroes who cannot sing,
The Huns gelded and feeding in a ring.
        Allen Tate: *More Sonnets at Christmas*, 1942

I   *The Apostles: Versailles, 1919*

They sat. They stood about.
They were estranged. The air,
As water curdles from clear,
Fleshed the silence. They sat.

They were appalled. The bells
In hollowed Europe spilt
To the gods of coin and salt.
The sea creaked with worked vessels.

II *The Lowlands of Holland*

Europe, the much-scarred, much-scoured terrain,
Its attested liberties, home-produce,
Labelled and looking up, invites use,
Stuffed with artistry and substantial gain:

Shrunken, magnified – (nest, holocaust) –
Not half innocent and not half undone;
Profiting from custom: its replete strewn
Cities such ample monuments to lost

Nations and generations: its cultural
Or trade skeletons such hand-picked bone:
Flaws in the best, revised science marks down:
Witness many devices; the few natural

Corruptions, graftings; witness classic falls;
(The dead subtracted; the greatest resigned;)
Witness earth fertilised, decently drained,
The sea decent again behind walls.

i

Slime; the residues of refined tears;
And, salt-bristled, blown on a drying sea,
The sunned and risen faces.
                                                There's Andromeda
Depicted in relief, after the fashion.

'His guarded eyes under his shielded brow'
Through poisonous baked sea-things Perseus
Goes – clogged sword, clear, aimless mirror –
With nothing to strike at or blind
                                        in the frothed shallows.

ii

Rivers bring down. The sea
Brings away;
Voids, sucks back, its pearls and auguries.
Eagles or vultures churn the fresh-made skies.

Over the statues, unchanging features
Of commerce and quaint love, soot lies.
Earth steams. The bull and the great mute swan
Strain into life with their notorious cries.

IV

Statesmen have known visions. And, not alone,
Artistic men prod dead men from their stone:
Some of us have heard the dead speak:
The dead are my obsession this week

But may be lifted away. In summer
Thunder may strike, or, as a tremor
Of remote adjustment, pass on the far side
From us: however deified and defied

By those it does strike. Many have died. Auschwitz,
Its furnace chambers and lime pits
Half-erased, is half-dead; a fable
Unbelievable in fatted marble.

There is, at times, some need to demonstrate
Jehovah's touchy methods, that create
The connoisseur of blood, the smitten man.
At times it seems not common to explain.

V   Ode on the loss of the 'Titanic'

Thriving against façades the ignorant sea
Souses our public baths, statues, waste ground:
Archaic earth-shaker, fresh enemy:
('The tables of exchange being overturned');

Drowns Babel in upheaval and display;
Unswerving, as were the admired multitudes
Silenced from time to time under its sway.
By all means let us appease the terse gods.

VI *The Martyrdom of Saint Sebastian*

Homage to Henry James

'But then face to face'

Naked, as if for swimming, the martyr
Catches his death in a little flutter
Of plain arrows. A grotesque situation,
But priceless, and harmless to the nation.

Consider such pains 'crystalline': then fine art
Persists where most crystals accumulate.
History can be scraped clean of its old price.
Engrossed in the cold blood of sacrifice,

The provident and self-healing gods
Destroy only to save. Well-stocked with foods,
Enlarged and deep-oiled, America
Detects music, apprehends the day-star

Where, sensitive and half-under a cloud,
Europe muddles her dreaming, is loud
And critical beneath the varied domes
Resonant with tribute and with commerce.

DOCTOR FAUSTUS

For it must needs be that offences come; but woe to
that man by whom the offence cometh.

I The Emperor's Clothes

A way of many ways: a god
Spirals in the pure steam of blood.
And gods – as men – rise from shut tombs
To a disturbance of small drums;

Immaculate plumage of the swan
The common wear. There is no-one
Afraid or overheard, no loud
Voice (though innocently loud).

II The Harpies

Having stood hungrily apart
From the gods' politic banquet,
Of all possible false gods
I fall to these gristled shades

That show everything, without lust;
And stumble upon their dead feast
By the torn *Warning To Bathers*
By the torn waters.

III   *Another Part of the Fable*

The Innocents have not flown;
Too legendary, they laugh;
The lewd uproarious wolf
Brings their house down.

A beast is slain, a beast thrives.
Fat blood squeaks on the sand.
A blinded god believes
That he is not blind.

A PASTORAL

Mobile, immaculate and austere,
The Pities, their fingers in every wound,
Assess the injured on the obscured frontier;
Cleanse with a kind of artistry the ground
Shared by War. Consultants in new tongues
Prove synonymous our separated wrongs.

We celebrate, fluently and at ease.
Traditional Furies, having thrust, hovered,
Now decently enough sustain Peace.
The unedifying nude dead are soon covered.
Survivors, still given to wandering, find
Their old loves, painted and re-aligned –

Queer, familiar, fostered by superb graft
On treasured foundations, these ideal features!
Men can move with purpose again, or drift,
According to direction. Here are statues
Darkened by laurel; and evergreen names;
Evidently-veiled griefs; impervious tombs.

ORPHEUS AND EURYDICE

Though there are wild dogs
    Infesting the roads
We have recitals, catalogues
    Of protected birds;

And the rare pale sun
    To water our days.
Men turn to savagery now or turn
    To the laws'

Immutable black and red.
    To be judged for his song,
Traversing the still-moist dead,
    The newly-stung,

Love goes, carrying compassion
    To the rawly-difficult;
His countenance, his hands' motion,
    Serene even to a fault.

IN PIAM MEMORIAM

I

Created purely from glass the saint stands,
Exposing his gifted quite empty hands
Like a conjurer about to begin,
A righteous man begging of righteous men.

II

In the sun lily-and-gold-coloured,
Filtering the cruder light, he has endured,
A feature for our regard; and will keep;
Of worldly purity the stained archetype.

III

The scummed pond twitches. The great holly-tree,
Emptied and shut, blows clear of wasting snow,
The common, puddled substance: beneath,
Like a revealed mineral, a new earth.

TO THE (SUPPOSED) PATRON

Prodigal of loves and barbecues,
Expert in the strangest faunas, at home
He considers the lilies, the rewards.
There is no substitute for a rich man.
At his first entering a new province
With new coin, music, the barest glancing
Of steel or gold suffices. There are many
Tremulous dreams secured under that head.
For his delight and his capacity
To absorb, freshly, the inside-succulence
Of untoughened sacrifice, his bronze agents
Speculate among convertible stones
And drink desert sand. That no mirage
Irritate his mild gaze, the lewd noonday
Is housed in cool places, and fountains
Salt the sparse haze. His flesh is made clean.
For the unfallen – the firstborn, or wise
Councillor – prepared vistas extend
As far as harvest; and idyllic death
Where fish at dawn ignite the powdery lake.

KING LOG

OVID IN THE THIRD REICH

non peccat, quaecumque potest peccasse negare,
   solaque famosam culpa professa facit.
      (Amores, III, xiv)

I love my work and my children. God
Is distant, difficult. Things happen.
Too near the ancient troughs of blood
Innocence is no earthly weapon.

I have learned one thing: not to look down
So much upon the damned. They, in their sphere,
Harmonize strangely with the divine
Love. I, in mine, celebrate the love-choir.

ANNUNCIATIONS

I

The Word has been abroad, is back, with a tanned look
From its subsistence in the stiffening-mire.
Cleansing has become killing, the reward
Touchable, overt, clean to the touch.
Now at a distance from the steam of beasts,
The loathly neckings and fat shook spawn
(Each specimen-jar fed with delicate spawn)
The searchers with the curers sit at meat
And are satisfied. Such precious things put down
And the flesh eased through turbulence the soul
Purples itself; each eye squats full and mild
While all who attend to fiddle or to harp
For betterment, flavour their decent mouths
With gobbets of the sweetest sacrifice.

O Love, subject of the mere diurnal grind,
Forever being pledged to be redeemed,
Expose yourself for charity; be assured
The body is but husk and excrement.
Enter these deaths according to the law,
O visited women, possessed sons! Foreign lusts
Infringe our restraints; the changeable
Soldiery have their goings-out and comings-in
Dying in abundance. Choicest beasts
Suffuse the gutters with their colourful blood.
Our God scatters corruption. Priests, martyrs,
Parade to this imperious theme: 'O Love,
You know what pains succeed; be vigilant; strive
To recognize the damned among your friends.'

LOCUST SONGS

To Allan Seager

THE EMBLEM

So with sweet oaths converting the salt earth
To yield, our fathers verged on Paradise:
Each to his own portion of Paradise,
Stung by the innocent venoms of the earth.

GOOD HUSBANDRY

Out of the foliage of sensual pride
Those teeming apples! Summer burned well
The dramatic flesh; made work for pride
Forking into the tender mouths of Hell

Heaped windfalls, pulp for the Gadarene
Squealers. This must be our reward:
To smell God writhing over the rich scene.
Gluttons for wrath, we stomach our reward.

SHILOH CHURCH, 1862: TWENTY-THREE THOUSAND

O stamping-ground of the shod Word! So hard
On the heels of the damned red-man we came,
Geneva's tribe, outlandish and abhorred –
Bland vistas milky with Jehovah's calm –

Who fell to feasting Nature, the glare
Of buzzards circling; cried to the grim sun
'Jehovah punish us!'; who went too far;
In deserts dropped the odd white turds of bone;

Whose passion was to find out God in this
His natural filth, voyeur of sacrifice, a slow
Bloody unearthing of the God-in-us.
But with what blood, and to what end, Shiloh?

I HAD HOPE WHEN VIOLENCE WAS CEAS'T

Dawnlight freezes against the east-wire.
The guards cough 'raus! 'raus! We flinch and grin,
Our flesh oozing towards its last outrage.
That which is taken from me is not mine.

SEPTEMBER SONG

born 19.6.32 – deported 24.9.42

Undesirable you may have been, untouchable
you were not. Not forgotten
or passed over at the proper time.

As estimated, you died. Things marched,
sufficient, to that end.
Just so much Zyklon and leather, patented
terror, so many routine cries.

(I have made
an elegy for myself it
is true)

September fattens on vines. Roses
flake from the wall. The smoke
of harmless fires drifts to my eyes.

This is plenty. This is more than enough.

AN ORDER OF SERVICE

He was the surveyor of his own ice-world,
Meticulous at the chosen extreme,
Though what he surveyed may have been nothing.

Let a man sacrifice himself, concede
His mortality and have done with it;
There is no end to that sublime appeal.

In such a light dismiss the unappealing
Blank of his gaze, hopelessly vigilant,
Dazzled by renunciation's glare.

THE HUMANIST

The *Venice* portrait: he
Broods, the achieved guest
Tired and word-perfect
At the Muses' table.

Virtue is virtù. These
Lips debate and praise –
Some rich aphorism;
A delicate white meat.

The commonplace hands once
Thick with Plato's blood
(Tasteless! tasteless!) are laid
Dryly against the robes.

FUNERAL MUSIC

William de la Pole, Duke of Suffolk: beheaded 1450
John Tiptoft, Earl of Worcester: beheaded 1470
Anthony Woodville, Earl Rivers: beheaded 1483

I

Processionals in the exemplary cave,
Benediction of shadows. Pomfret. London.
The voice fragrant with mannered humility,
With an equable contempt for this World,
'In honorem Trinitatis'. Crash. The head
Struck down into a meaty conduit of blood.
So these dispose themselves to receive each
Pentecostal blow from axe or seraph,
Spattering block-straw with mortal residue.
Psalteries whine through the empyrean. Fire
Flares in the pit, ghosting upon stone
Creatures of such rampant state, vacuous
Ceremony of possession, restless
Habitation, no man's dwelling-place.

For whom do we scrape our tribute of pain –
For none but the ritual king? We meditate
A rueful mystery; we are dying
To satisfy fat Caritas, those
Wiped jaws of stone. (Suppose all reconciled
By silent music; imagine the future
Flashed back at us, like steel against sun,
Ultimate recompense.) Recall the cold
Of Towton on Palm Sunday before dawn,
Wakefield, Tewkesbury: fastidious trumpets
Shrilling into the ruck; some trampled
Acres, parched, sodden or blanched by sleet,
Stuck with strange-postured dead. Recall the wind's
Flurrying, darkness over the human mire.

3

They bespoke doomsday and they meant it by
God, their curved metal rimming the low ridge.
But few appearances are like this. Once
Every five hundred years a comet's
Over-riding stillness might reveal men
In such array, livid and featureless,
With England crouched beastwise beneath it all.
'Oh, that old northern business . . .' A field
After battle utters its own sound
Which is like nothing on earth, but is earth.
Blindly the questing snail, vulnerable
Mole emerge, blindly we lie down, blindly
Among carnage the most delicate souls
Tup in their marriage-blood, gasping 'Jesus'.

4

Let mind be more precious than soul; it will not
Endure. Soul grasps its price, begs its own peace,
Settles with tears and sweat, is possibly
Indestructible. That I can believe.
Though I would scorn the mere instinct of faith,
Expediency of assent, if I dared,
What I dare not is a waste history
Or void rule. Averroes, old heathen,
If only you had been right, if Intellect
Itself were absolute law, sufficient grace,
Our lives could be a myth of captivity
Which we might enter: an unpeopled region
Of ever new-fallen snow, a palace blazing
With perpetual silence as with torches.

63

As with torches we go, at wild Christmas,
When we revel in our atonement
Through thirty feasts of unction and slaughter,
What is that but the soul's winter sleep?
So many things rest under consummate
Justice as though trumpets purified law,
Spikenard were the real essence of remorse.
The sky gathers up darkness. When we chant
'Ora, ora pro nobis' it is not
Seraphs who descend to pity but ourselves.
Those righteously-accused those vengeful
Racked on articulate looms indulge us
With lingering shows of pain, a flagrant
Tenderness of the damned for their own flesh:

My little son, when you could command marvels
Without mercy, outstare the wearisome
Dragon of sleep, I rejoiced above all –
A stranger well-received in your kingdom.
On those pristine fields I saw humankind
As it was named by the Father; fabulous
Beasts rearing in stillness to be blessed.
The world's real cries reached there, turbulence
From remote storms, rumour of solitudes,
A composed mystery. And so it ends.
Some parch for what they were; others are made
Blind to all but one vision, their necessity
To be reconciled. I believe in my
Abandonment, since it is what I have.

'Prowess, vanity, mutual regard,
It seemed I stared at them, they at me.
That was the gorgon's true and mortal gaze:
Averted conscience turned against itself.'
A hawk and a hawk-shadow. 'At noon,
As the armies met, each mirrored the other;
Neither was outshone. So they flashed and vanished
And all that survived them was the stark ground
Of this pain. I made no sound, but once
I stiffened as though a remote cry
Had heralded my name. It was nothing . . .'
Reddish ice tinged the reeds; dislodged, a few
Feathers drifted across; carrion birds
Strutted upon the armour of the dead.

Not as we are but as we must appear,
Contractual ghosts of pity; not as we
Desire life but as they would have us live,
Set apart in timeless colloquy:
So it is required; so we bear witness,
Despite ourselves, to what is beyond us,
Each distant sphere of harmony forever
Poised, unanswerable. If it is without
Consequence when we vaunt and suffer, or
If it is not, all echoes are the same
In such eternity. Then tell me, love,
How that should comfort us – or anyone
Dragged half-unnerved out of this worldly place,
Crying to the end 'I have not finished'.

FOUR POEMS REGARDING
THE ENDURANCE
OF POETS

MEN ARE A MOCKERY OF ANGELS

i.m. Tommaso Campanella, priest and poet

Some days a shadow through
The high window shares my
Prison. I watch a slug
Scale the glinting pit-side
Of its own slime. The cries
As they come are mine; then
God's: my justice, wounds, love,
Derisive light, bread, filth.

To lie here in my strange
Flesh while glutted Torment
Sleeps, stained with its prompt food,
Is a joy past all care
Of the world, for a time.
But we are commanded
To rise, when, in silence,
I would compose my voice.

A PRAYER TO THE SUN

i.m. Miguel Hernandez

i
Darkness
above all things
the Sun
makes
rise

ii
Vultures
salute their meat
at noon
(Hell is
silent)

iii
Blind Sun
our ravager
bless us
so that
we sleep.

'DOMAINE PUBLIC'

i.m. Robert Desnos, died Terezin Camp, 1945

For reading I can recommend
   the Fathers. How they
cultivate the corrupting flesh:

toothsome contemplation: cleanly
   maggots churning spleen
to milk. For exercise, prolonged

suppression of much improper
   speech from proper tombs.
If the ground opens, should men's mouths

open also? 'I am nothing
   if not saved now!' or
'Christ, what a pantomime!' The days

of the week are seven pits. Look,
   Seigneur, again we
resurrect and the judges come.

A Valediction to Osip Mandelshtam

Difficult friend, I would have preferred
You to them. The dead keep their sealed lives
And again I am too late. Too late
The salutes, dust-clouds and brazen cries.

Images rear from desolation
Look . . . ruins upon a plain . . .
A few men glare at their hands; others
Grovel for food in the roadside field.

Tragedy has all under regard.
It will not touch us but it is there –
Flawless, insatiate – hard summer sky
Feasting on this, reaching its own end.

THE IMAGINATIVE LIFE

Evasive souls, of whom the wise lose track,
Die in each night, who, with their day-tongues, sift
The waking-taste of manna or of blood:

The raw magi, part-barbarians,
Entranced by demons and desert frost,
By the irregular visions of a god,

Suffragans of the true seraphs. Lust
Writhes, is dumb savage and in their way
As a virulence natural to the earth.

Renewed glories batten on the poor bones;
Gargantuan mercies whetted by a scent
Of mortal sweat: as though the sleeping flesh

Adored by Furies, stirred, yawned, were driven
In mid-terror to purging and delight.
As though the dead had *Finis* on their brows.

THE ASSISI FRAGMENTS

To G. Wilson Knight

1

Lion and lioness, the mild
Inflammable beasts,
At their precise peril kept
Distance and repose –
And there the serpent
Innocently shone its head.

2

So the hawk had its pursuit. So Death
Opened its childish eyes. So the angels
Overcame Adam: he was defiled
By balm. Creator, and creature made
Of unnatural earth, he howled
To the raven *find me;* to the wolf
Eat, my brother; and to the fire *I am clean.*

HISTORY AS POETRY

Poetry as salutation; taste
Of Pentecost's ashen feast. Blue wounds.
The tongue's atrocities. Poetry
Unearths from among the speechless dead

Lazarus mystified, common man
Of death. The lily rears its gouged face
From the provided loam. Fortunate
Auguries; whirrings; tarred golden dung:

'A resurgence' as they say. The old
Laurels wagging with the new: Selah!
Thus laudable the trodden bone thus
Unanswerable the knack of tongues.

SOLILOQUIES

THE STONE MAN

To Charles Causley

Recall, now, the omens of childhood:
The nettle-clump and rank elder-tree;
The stones waiting in the mason's yard:

Half-recognized kingdom of the dead:
A deeper landscape lit by distant
Flashings from their journey. At nightfall

My father scuffed clay into the house.
He set his boots on the bleak iron
Of the hearth; ate, drank, unbuckled, slept.

I leaned to the lamp; the pallid moths
Clipped its glass, made an autumnal sound.
Words clawed my mind as though they had smelt

Revelation's flesh . . . So, with an ease
That is dreadful, I summon all back.
The sun bellows over its parched swarms.

What I lost was not a part of this.
The dark-blistered foxgloves, wet berries
Glinting from shadow, small ferns and stones,

Seem fragments, in the observing mind,
Of its ritual power. Old age
Singles them out as though by first-light,

As though a still-life, preserving some
Portion of the soul's feast, went with me
Everywhere, to be hung in strange rooms,

Loneliness being what it is. If
I knew the exact coin for tribute,
Defeat might be bought, processional

Silence gesture its tokens of earth
At my mouth: as in the great death-songs
Of Propertius (although he died young).

COWAN BRIDGE

At the site of 'Lowood School'

A lost storm in this temperate place;
The silent direction;
Some ash-trees and foam-patched
Alders at the beck.

All the seasons absorbed
As by a child, safe from rain,
Crouched in the dank
Stench of an elder-bush.

So much that was not justice,
So much that is;
The vulnerable pieties
Not willingly let die;
By chance unmolested
The modesty of her rage.

FANTASIA ON 'HORBURY'

J.B.D. 1859

Dry walls, and nettles battered by the dust,
Odours from gathered water, muddled storm-clouds
Disastrous over the manufactured West Riding.

Mind – a fritter of excrement; step
Aside, step aside, sir! Ah, but a priest
In his prime watches where he goes. He goes

To tender his confession. Forgiveness
Journeys towards him like a brisk traveller
On the same road. Is this Horbury?

Yes: and he will perpetuate this refuge.
Yes: and he will weaken, scribbling, at the end,
Of unspeakable desolation. Really? Good Lord!

Consider him thus animated,
That outworn piety and those plush tunes
Restored for the sake of a paradox

And the too-fashionable North. Or, again,
Consider him catspawed by an indolent poem,
This place not of his choosing, this menace

From concave stormlight a freak suggestion . . .
These heads of nettles lopped into the dust . . .

THREE BAROQUE MEDITATIONS

I

Do words make up the majesty
Of man, and his justice
Between the stones and the void?

How they watch us, the demons
Plugging their dumb wounds! When
Exorcized they shrivel yet thrive.

An owl plunges to its tryst
With a field-mouse in the sharp night.
My fire squeals and lies still.

Minerva, receive this hard
Praise: I speak well of Death;
I confess to the priest in me;

I am shadowed by the wise bird
Of necessity, the lithe
Paradigm Sleep-and-Kill.

Anguish bloated by the replete scream.
Flesh of abnegation: the poem
Moves grudgingly to its extreme form,

Vulnerable, to the lamp's fierce head
Of well-trimmed light. In darkness outside,
Foxes and rain-sleeked stones and the dead –

Aliens of such a theme – endure
Until I could cry 'Death! Death!' as though
To exacerbate that suave power;

But refrain. For I am circumspect,
Lifting the spicy lid of my tact
To sniff at the myrrh. It is perfect

In its impalpable bitterness,
Scent of a further country where worse
Furies promenade and bask their claws.

So white I was, he would have me cry
'Unclean!' murderously
To heal me with far-fetched blood.

I writhed to conceive of him.
I clawed to becalm him.
Some nights, I witnessed his face in sleep

And dreamed of my father's
House. (By day he professed languages –
Disciplines of languages) –

By day I cleansed my pink tongue
From its nightly prowl, its vixen-skill,
His sacramental mouth

That justified my flesh
And moved well among women
In nuances and imperatives.

This was the poet of a people's
Love. I hated him. He weeps,
Solemnizing his loss.

THE SONGBOOK
OF
SEBASTIAN ARRURRUZ

Sebastian Arrurruz: 1868–1922

I

Ten years without you. For so it happens.
Days make their steady progress, a routine
That is merciful and attracts nobody.

Already, like a disciplined scholar,
I piece fragments together, past conjecture
Establishing true sequences of pain;

For so it is proper to find value
In a bleak skill, as in the thing restored:
The long-lost words of choice and valediction.

i

'One cannot lose what one has not possessed'.
So much for that abrasive gem.
I can lose what I want. I want you.

ii

Oh my dear one, I shall grieve for you
For the rest of my life with slightly
Varying cadence, oh my dear one.

iii

Half-mocking the half-truth, I note
'The wild brevity of sensual love'.
I am shaken, even by that.

iv

It is to him I write, it is to her
I speak in contained silence. Will they be touched
By the unfamiliar passion between them?

What other men do with other women
Is for me neither orgy nor sacrament
Nor a language of foreign candour

But is mere occasion or chance distance
Out of which you might move and speak my name
As I speak yours, bargaining with sleep's

Miscellaneous gods for as much
As I can have: an alien landscape,
The dream where you are always to be found.

4

A workable fancy. Old petulant
Sorrow comes back to us, metamorphosed
And semi-precious. Fortuitous amber.
As though this recompensed our deprivation.
See how each fragment kindles as we turn it,
At the end, into the light of appraisal.

5

Love, oh my love, it will come
Sure enough! A storm
Broods over the dry earth all day.
At night the shutters throb in its downpour.

The metaphor holds; is a snug house.
You are outside, lost somewhere. I find myself
Devouring verses of stranger passion
And exile. The exact words

Are fed into my blank hunger for you.

I imagine, as I imagine us
Each time more stylized more lovingly
Detailed, that I am not myself
But someone I might have been: sexless,
Indulgent about art, relishing
Let us say the well-schooled
Postures of *St Anthony* or *St Jerome*,
Those peaceful hermaphrodite dreams
Through which the excess of memory
Pursues its own abstinence.

There would have been things to say, quietness
That could feed on our lust, refreshed
Trivia, the occurrences of the day;
And at night my tongue in your furrow.

Without you I am mocked by courtesies
And chat, where satisfied women push
Dutifully toward some unneeded guest
Desirable features of conversation.

[*1922*]

So, remotely, in your part of the world:
the ripe glandular blooms, and cypresses
shivering with heat (which we have borne
also, in our proper ways) I turn my mind
towards delicate pillage, the provenance
of shards glazed and unglazed, the three
kinds of surviving grain. I hesitate amid
circumstantial disasters. I gaze at the
authentic dead.

Roughly-silvered leaves that are the snow
On Ararat seen through those leaves.
The sun lays down a foliage of shade.

A drinking-fountain pulses its head
Two or three inches from the troughed stone.
An old woman sucks there, gripping the rim.

Why do I have to relive, even now,
Your mouth, and your hand running over me
Deft as a lizard, like a sinew of water?

You ventured occasionally –
As though this were another's house –
Not intimate but an acquaintance
Flaunting her modest claim; like one
Idly commiserated by new-mated
Lovers rampant in proper delight
When all their guests have gone.

[*1921*]

Scarcely speaking: it becomes as a
Coolness between neighbours. Often
There is this orgy of sleep. I wake
To caress propriety with odd words
And enjoy abstinence in a vocation
Of now-almost-meaningless despair.

MERCIAN HYMNS

I

King of the perennial holly-groves, the riven sand-
stone: overlord of the M5: architect of the his-
toric rampart and ditch, the citadel at Tamworth,
the summer hermitage in Holy Cross: guardian of
the Welsh Bridge and the Iron Bridge: contractor
to the desirable new estates: saltmaster: money-
changer: commissioner for oaths: martyrologist:
the friend of Charlemagne.

'I liked that,' said Offa, 'sing it again.'

II

A pet-name, a common name. Best-selling brand, curt
   graffito. A laugh; a cough. A syndicate. A specious
   gift. Scoffed-at horned phonograph.

The starting-cry of a race. A name to conjure with.

III

On the morning of the crowning we chorused our re-
mission from school. It was like Easter: hankies
and gift-mugs approved by his foreign gaze, the
village-lintels curlered with paper flags.

We gaped at the car-park of 'The Stag's Head' where a
bonfire of beer-crates and holly-boughs whistled
above the tar. And the chef stood there, a king in
his new-risen hat, sealing his brisk largesse with
'any mustard?'

IV

.

I was invested in mother-earth, the crypt of roots
and endings. Child's-play. I abode there, bided my
time: where the mole

shouldered the clogged wheel, his gold solidus; where
dry-dust badgers thronged the Roman flues, the
long-unlooked-for mansions of our tribe.

V

So much for the elves' wergild, the true governance
of England, the gaunt warrior-gospel armoured in
engraved stone. I wormed my way heavenward for
ages amid barbaric ivy, scrollwork of fern.

Exile or pilgrim set me once more upon that ground:
my rich and desolate childhood. Dreamy, smug-faced,
sick on outings—I who was taken to be a king of
some kind, a prodigy, a maimed one.

VI

The princes of Mercia were badger and raven. Thrall
to their freedom, I dug and hoarded. Orchards
fruited above clefts. I drank from honeycombs of
chill sandstone.

'A boy at odds in the house, lonely among brothers.'
But I, who had none, fostered a strangeness; gave
myself to unattainable toys.

Candles of gnarled resin, apple-branches, the tacky
mistletoe. 'Look' they said and again 'look.' But
I ran slowly; the landscape flowed away, back to
its source.

In the schoolyard, in the cloakrooms, the children
boasted their scars of dried snot; wrists and
knees garnished with impetigo.

VII

Gasholders, russet among fields. Milldams, marlpools that lay unstirring. Eel-swarms. Coagulations of frogs: once, with branches and half-bricks, he battered a ditchful; then sidled away from the stillness and silence.

Ceolred was his friend and remained so, even after the day of the lost fighter: a biplane, already obsolete and irreplaceable, two inches of heavy snub silver. Ceolred let it spin through a hole in the classroom-floorboards, softly, into the rat-droppings and coins.

After school he lured Ceolred, who was sniggering with fright, down to the old quarries, and flayed him. Then, leaving Ceolred, he journeyed for hours, calm and alone, in his private derelict sandlorry named *Albion*.

VIII

The mad are predators. Too often lately they harbour
   against us. A novel heresy exculpates all maimed
   souls. Abjure it! I am the King of Mercia, and
   I know.

Threatened by phone-calls at midnight, venomous let-
   ters, forewarned I have thwarted their imminent
   devices.

Today I name them; tomorrow I shall express the new
   law. I dedicate my awakening to this matter.

IX

The strange church smelled a bit 'high', of censers
   and polish. The strange curate was just as ap-
   propriate: he took off into the marriage-service.
   No-one cared to challenge that gambit.

Then he dismissed you, and the rest of us followed,
   sheepish next-of-kin, to the place without the
   walls: spoil-heaps of chrysanths dead in their
   plastic macs, eldorado of washstand-marble.

Embarrassed, we dismissed ourselves: the three mute
   great-aunts borne away down St Chad's Garth in
   a stiff-backed Edwardian Rolls.

I unburden the saga of your burial, my dear. You had
   lived long enough to see things 'nicely settled'.

X

He adored the desk, its brown-oak inlaid with ebony,
   assorted prize pens, the seals of gold and base
   metal into which he had sunk his name.

It was there that he drew upon grievances from the
   people; attended to signatures and retributions;
   forgave the death-howls of his rival. And there
   he exchanged gifts with the Muse of History.

What should a man make of remorse, that it might
   profit his soul? Tell me. Tell everything to
   Mother, darling, and God bless.

He swayed in sunlight, in mild dreams. He tested the
   little pears. He smeared catmint on his palm for
   his cat Smut to lick. He wept, attempting to mas-
   ter *ancilla* and *servus*.

XI

Coins handsome as Nero's; of good substance and
weight. *Offa Rex* resonant in silver, and the
names of his moneyers. They struck with account-
able tact. They could alter the king's face.

Exactness of design was to deter imitation; mutil-
ation if that failed. Exemplary metal, ripe for
commerce. Value from a sparse people, scrapers of
salt-pans and byres.

Swathed bodies in the long ditch; one eye upstaring.
It is safe to presume, here, the king's anger. He
reigned forty years. Seasons touched and retouch-
ed the soil.

Heathland, new-made watermeadow. Charlock, marsh-
marigold. Crepitant oak forest where the boar
furrowed black mould, his snout intimate with
worms and leaves.

XII

Their spades grafted through the variably-resistant soil. They clove to the hoard. They ransacked epiphanies, vertebrae of the chimera, armour of wild bees' larvae. They struck the fire-dragon's faceted skin.

The men were paid to caulk water-pipes. They brewed and pissed amid splendour; their latrine seethed its estuary through nettles. They are scattered to your collations, moldywarp.

It is autumn. Chestnut-boughs clash their inflamed leaves. The garden festers for attention: telluric cultures enriched with shards, corms, nodules, the sunk solids of gravity. I have accrued a golden and stinking blaze.

XIII

Trim the lamp; polish the lens; draw, one by one, rare
coins to the light. Ringed by its own lustre, the
masterful head emerges, kempt and jutting, out of
England's well. Far from his underkingdom of crin-
oid and crayfish, the rune-stone's province, *Rex
Totius Anglorum Patriae,* coiffured and ageless,
portrays the self-possession of his possession,
cushioned on a legend.

XIV

Dismissing reports and men, he put pressure on the
  wax, blistered it to a crest. He threatened male-
  factors with ash from his noon cigar.

When the sky cleared above Malvern, he lingered in
  his orchard; by the quiet hammer-pond. Trout-fry
  simmered there, translucent, as though forming the
  water's underskin. He had a care for natural min-
  utiae. What his gaze touched was his tenderness.
  Woodlice sat pellet-like in the cracked bark and
  a snail sugared its new stone.

At dinner, he relished the mockery of drinking his
  family's health. He did this whenever it suited
  him, which was not often.

XV

Tutting, he wrenched at a snarled root of dead crab-
apple. It rose against him. In brief cavort he was
Cernunnos, the branched god, lightly concussed.

He divided his realm. It lay there like a dream. An
ancient land, full of strategy. Ramparts of com-
post pioneered by red-helmeted worms. Hemlock in
ambush, night-soil, tetanus. A wasps' nest en-
sconced in the hedge-bank, a reliquary or wrapped
head, the corpse of Cernunnos pitching dayward
its feral horns.

XVI

Clash of salutation. As keels thrust into shingle.
Ambassadors, pilgrims. What is carried over? The
Frankish gift, two-edged, regaled with slaughter.

The sword is in the king's hands; the crux a crafts-
man's triumph. Metal effusing its own fragrance,
a variety of balm. And other miracles, other
exchanges.

Shafts from the winter sun homing upon earth's rim.
Christ's mass: in the thick of a snowy forest the
flickering evergreen fissured with light.

Attributes assumed, retribution entertained. What is
borne amongst them? Too much or too little. In-
dulgences of bartered acclaim; an expenditure, a
hissing. Wine, urine and ashes.

XVII

He drove at evening through the hushed Vosges. The
car radio, glimmering, received broken utterance
from the horizon of storms . . .

'God's honour—our bikes touched; he skidded and came
off.' 'Liar.' A timid father's protective bellow.
Disfigurement of a village-king. 'Just look at
the bugger . . .'

His maroon GT chanted then overtook. He lavished on
the high valleys its *haleine*.

XVIII

At Pavia, a visitation of some sorrow. Boethius'
dungeon. He shut his eyes, gave rise to a tower
out of the earth. He willed the instruments of
violence to break upon meditation. Iron buckles
gagged; flesh leaked rennet over them; the men
stooped, disentangled the body.

He wiped his lips and hands. He strolled back to the
car, with discreet souvenirs for consolation and
philosophy. He set in motion the furtherance of
his journey. To watch the Tiber foaming out
much blood.

XIX

Behind the thorn-trees thin smoke, scutch-grass or wattle smouldering. At this distance it is hard to tell. Far cries impinge like the faint tinking of iron.

We have a kitchen-garden riddled with toy-shards, with splinters of habitation. The children shriek and scavenge, play havoc. They incinerate boxes, rags and old tyres. They haul a sodden log, hung with soft shields of fungus, and launch it upon the flames.

XX

Primeval heathland spattered with the bones of mice
and birds; where adders basked and bees made pro-
vision, mantling the inner walls of their burh:

Coiled entrenched England: brickwork and paintwork
stalwart above hacked marl. The clashing prim-
ary colours—'Ethandune', 'Catraeth', 'Maldon',
'Pengwern'. Steel against yew and privet. Fresh
dynasties of smiths.

XXI

Cohorts of charabancs fanfared Offa's province and
his concern, negotiating the by-ways from Teme
to Trent. Their windshields dripped butterflies.
Stranded on hilltops they signalled with plumes
of steam. Twilight menaced the land. The young
women wept and surrendered.

Still, everyone was cheerful, heedless in such days:
at summer weekends dipping into valleys beyond
Mercia's dyke. Tea was enjoyed, by lakesides where
all might fancy carillons of real Camelot vib-
rating through the silent water.

Gradually, during the years, deciduous velvet peeled
from evergreen albums and during the years more
treasures were mislaid: the harp-shaped brooches,
the nuggets of fool's gold.

XXII

We ran across the meadow scabbed with cow-dung, past
the crab-apple trees and camouflaged nissen hut.
It was curfew-time for our war-band.

At home the curtains were drawn. The wireless boomed
its commands. I loved the battle-anthems and the
gregarious news.

Then, in the earthy shelter, warmed by a blue-glassed
storm-lantern, I huddled with stories of dragon-
tailed airships and warriors who took wing im-
mortal as phantoms.

XXIII

In tapestries, in dreams, they gathered, as it was en-
acted, the return, the re-entry of transcendence
into this sublunary world. *Opus Anglicanum*, their
stringent mystery riddled by needles: the silver
veining, the gold leaf, voluted grape-vine, master-
works of treacherous thread.

They trudged out of the dark, scraping their boots
free from lime-splodges and phlegm. They munched
cold bacon. The lamps grew plump with oily re-
liable light.

XXIV

Itinerant through numerous domains, of his lord's
retinue, to Compostela. Then home for a lifetime
amid West Mercia this master-mason as I envisage
him, intent to pester upon tympanum and chancel-
arch his moody testament, confusing warrior with
lion, dragon-coils, tendrils of the stony vine.

Where best to stand? Easter sunrays catch the ob-
lique face of Adam scrumping through leaves; pale
spree of evangelists and, there, a cross Christ
mumming child Adam out of Hell

('Et exspecto resurrectionem mortuorum' dust in the
eyes, on clawing wings, and lips)

XXV

Brooding on the eightieth letter of *Fors Clavigera*,
 I speak this in memory of my grandmother, whose
 childhood and prime womanhood were spent in the
 nailer's darg.

The nailshop stood back of the cottage, by the fold.
 It reeked stale mineral sweat. Sparks had furred
 its low roof. In dawn-light the troughed water
 floated a damson-bloom of dust—

not to be shaken by posthumous clamour. It is one
 thing to celebrate the 'quick forge', another
 to cradle a face hare-lipped by the searing wire.

Brooding on the eightieth letter of *Fors Clavigera*,
 I speak this in memory of my grandmother, whose
 childhood and prime womanhood were spent in the
 nailer's darg.

XXVI

Fortified in their front parlours, at Yuletide men
are the more murderous. Drunk, they defy battle-
axes, bellow of whale-bone and dung.

Troll-wives, groaners in sweetness, tooth-bewitchers,
you too must purge for the surfeit of England—
who have scattered peppermint and confetti, your
hundreds-and-thousands.

XXVII

'Now when King Offa was alive and dead', they were
all there, the funereal gleemen: papal legate and
rural dean; Merovingian car-dealers, Welsh mercen-
aries; a shuffle of house-carls.

He was defunct. They were perfunctory. The ceremony
stood acclaimed. The mob received memorial vouch-
ers and signs.

After that shadowy, thrashing midsummer hail-storm,
Earth lay for a while, the ghost-bride of livid
Thor, butcher of strawberries, and the shire-tree
dripped red in the arena of its uprooting.

XXVIII

Processes of generation; deeds of settlement. The urge to marry well; wit to invest in the properties of healing-springs. Our children and our children's children, o my masters.

Tracks of ancient occupation. Frail ironworks rusting in the thorn-thicket. Hearthstones; charred lullabies. A solitary axe-blow that is the echo of a lost sound.

Tumult recedes as though into the long rain. Groves of legendary holly; silverdark the ridged gleam.

XXIX

'Not strangeness, but strange likeness. Obstinate,
   outclassed forefathers, I too concede, I am your
   staggeringly-gifted child.'

So, murmurous, he withdrew from them. Gran lit the
   gas, his dice whirred in the ludo-cup, he entered
   into the last dream of Offa the King.

XXX

And it seemed, while we waited, he began to walk to-
    wards us   he vanished

he left behind coins, for his lodging, and traces of
    red mud.

FUNERAL MUSIC
an essay

In this sequence I was attempting a florid grim music broken by grunts and shrieks. Ian Nairn's description of Eltham Palace as 'a perfect example of the ornate heartlessness of much mid-fifteenth-century architecture, especially court architecture'[1] is pertinent, though I did not read Nairn until after the sequence had been completed. The Great Hall was made for Edward IV. *Funeral Music* could be called a commination and an alleluia for the period popularly but inexactly known as the Wars of the Roses. It bears an oblique dedication. In the case of Suffolk the word 'beheaded' is a retrospective aggrandisement; he was in fact butchered across the gunwale of a skiff. Tiptoft enjoyed a degree of ritual, commanding that he should be decapitated in three strokes 'in honour of the Trinity'. This was a nice compounding of orthodox humility and unorthodox arrogance. Did Tiptoft see himself as Everyman's emblem or as the unique figure preserved in the tableau of his own death? As historic characters Suffolk, Worcester and Rivers haunt the mind vulnerable alike to admiration and scepticism. Was Suffolk – the friend of the captive poet Charles d'Orleans and an advocate of peace with France – a visionary or a racketeer? The Woodville clan invites irritated dismissal: pushful, time-serving, it was really not its business to produce a man like Earl Rivers, who was something of a religious mystic and whose translation, *The Dictes and Sayings of the Philosophers*, was the first book printed in England by Caxton. Suffolk and Rivers were poets, though quite tame. Tiptoft, patron of humanist scholars, was known as the Butcher of England because of his pleasure in varying the accepted postures of judicial death.

Admittedly, the sequence avoids shaping these characters and events into any overt narrative or dramatic structure. The whole inference, though, has value if it gives a key to the ornate and heartless music punctuated by mutterings, blasphemies and cries for help.

There is a distant fury of battle. Without attempting factual detail, I had in mind the Battle of Towton, fought on Palm Sunday, 1461. It is now customary to play down the violence of the Wars of the Roses and to present them as dynastic skirmishes fatal, perhaps, to the old aristocracy but generally of small concern to the common people and without much effect on the economic routines of the kingdom. Statistically, this may be arguable; imaginatively, the Battle of Towton itself commands one's belated witness. In the accounts of the contemporary chroniclers it was a holocaust. Some scholars have suggested that the claims were exaggerated, although the military historian, Colonel A. H. Burne, argues convincingly for the reasonableness of the early estimates. He reckons that over twenty-six thousand men died at Towton and remarks that 'the scene must have beggared description and its very horror probably deterred the survivors from passing on stories of the fight'.[2] Even so, one finds the chronicler of Croyland Abbey writing that the blood of the slain lay caked with the snow which covered the ground and that, when the snow melted, the blood flowed along the furrows and ditches for a distance of two or three miles.[3]

[1] Ian Nairn, *Nairn's London* (Penguin, 1966), p. 208
[2] A. H. Burne, *The Battlefields of England* (Methuen, 1950), p. 100
[3] Cited by C. R. Markham, *The Yorkshire Archaeological and Topographical Journal*, Vol. 10 (1889), p. 13

ON 'MERCIAN HYMNS'

The historical King Offa reigned over Mercia (and the greater part of England south of the Humber) in the years AD 757–796. During early medieval times he was already becoming a creature of legend. The Offa who figures in this sequence might perhaps most usefully be regarded as the presiding genius of the West Midlands, his dominion enduring from the middle of the eighth century until the middle of the twentieth (and possibly beyond). The indication of such a timespan will, I trust, explain and to some extent justify a number of anachronisms.

I have a duty to acknowledge that the authorities cited in these notes might properly object to their names being used in so unscholarly and fantastic a context. I have no wish to compromise the accurate scholarship of others. Having taken over certain statements and references from my reading and having made them a part of the idiom of this sequence, I believe that I should acknowledge the sources. I have specified those debts of which I am aware. Possibly there are others of which I am unaware. If that is so I regret the oversight.

The title of the sequence is a suggestion taken from

Sweet's Anglo-Saxon Reader, Oxford (Twelfth Edition, 1950), pp. 170–80. A less-immediate precedent is provided by the Latin prose-hymns or canticles of the early Christian Church. See Frederick Brittain, ed., *The Penguin Book of Latin Verse*, Harmondsworth (1962), pp. xvii, lv.

II: 'a common name' cf. W. F. Bolton, *A History of Anglo-Latin Literature 597–1066*, Princeton (1967), I, p. 191: 'But Offa is a common name'.

IV: 'I was invested in mother-earth'. To the best of my recollection, the expression 'to invest in mother-earth' was the felicitous (and correct) definition of 'yird' given by Mr Michael Hordern in the programme *Call My Bluff* televised on BBC 2 on Thursday January 29th 1970.

V: 'wergild': 'the price set upon a man according to his rank' (O.E.D.) cf. D. Whitelock, *The Beginnings of English Society*, Harmondsworth (1965 edition), ch. 5.

XI: '*Offa Rex*': an inscription on his coins. See J. J. North, *English Hammered Coinage*, London (1963), I, pp. 52–60 and Plate III.

XIII: '*Rex Totius Anglorum Patriae*': 'King of the Whole Country of the English'. See Christopher Brooke, *The Saxon and Norman Kings*, London (1967 edition), p. 200.

XV: 'Cernunnos': cf. *Larousse Encyclopedia of Mythology*, London (1960 edition), pp. 235, 244, 246–8.

XVII: '*haleine*': cf. *La Chanson de Roland*, ed.

F. Whitehead, Oxford (1942), 1789, 'Ço dist li reis: "Cel corn ad lunge aleine." '

XVIII: 'for consolation and philosophy': the allusion is to the title of Boethius' great meditation, though it is doubtless an excess of scruple to point this out.

'To watch the Tiber foaming out much blood': adapted from Vergil, *Aeneid*, VI, 87, 'et Thybrim multo spumantem sanguine cerno'.

XX: 'Ethandune', 'Catraeth', 'Maldon', 'Pengwern': in this context supposedly the names of English suburban dwellings. Ethandune = the Battle of Edington (Wilts), AD 878; Catraeth = the Battle of Catterick, late sixth century; Maldon = the Battle of Maldon, AD 991; Pengwern (Shrewsbury), capital of the Princes of Powys, taken by Offa, AD 779. See Anthony Conran, ed., *The Penguin Book of Welsh Verse*, Harmondsworth (1967), pp. 24–30, 75–78, 90–93; Richard Hamer, ed., *A Choice of Anglo-Saxon Verse*, London (1970), pp. 48–69; A. H. Smith, ed., *The Parker Chronicle*, London (Third Edition, 1951), pp. 31–2.

XXIII: '*Opus Anglicanum*': the term is properly applicable to English embroidery of the period AD 1250–1350, though the craft was already famous some centuries earlier. See A. G. I. Christie, *English Medieval Embroidery*, Oxford (1938), pp. 1–2. In XXIV and XXV I have, with considerable impropriety, extended the term to apply to English Romanesque sculpture and to utilitarian metal-work of the nineteenth century.

XXIV: for the association of Compostela with West Midlands sculpture of the twelfth century I am indebted to G. Zarnecki, *Later English Romanesque Sculpture*, London (1953), esp. pp. 9–15, 'The Herefordshire School'.

'Et exspecto resurrectionem mortuorum': a debt to Olivier Messiaen, his music 'for orchestra of woodwind, brass and metallic percussion'.

XXV: 'the eightieth letter of *Fors Clavigera*'. See *The Works of John Ruskin*, London (1903–1912), XXIX, pp. 170–180.

'darg': 'a day's work, the task of a day . . .' (O.E.D.). Ruskin employs the word, here and elsewhere.

'quick forge': see W. Shakespeare, *Henry V*, V, Chorus, 23. The phrase requires acknowledgment but the source has no bearing on the poem.

'wire': I seem not to have been strictly accurate. Hand-made nails were forged from rods. Wire was used for the 'French nails' made by machine. But: 'wire' = 'metal wrought into the form of a slender rod or thread' (O.E.D.).

XXVII: 'Now when King Offa was alive and dead' is based on a ritual phrase used of various kings though not, as far as I am aware, of Offa himself. See Christopher Brooke, *op. cit*, p. 39; R. H. M. Dolley, ed., *Anglo-Saxon Coins: Studies Presented to F. M. Stenton*, London (1961), p. 220.